DATE DUE			

Basic Domestic Pet Library

Aquarium Beautiful
A Complete and Up-to-Date Guide

Approved by the A.S.P.C.A.

A. van den Nieuwenhuizen

Published in association with T.F.H. Publications, Inc.,
the world's largest and most respected publisher of pet literature

Chelsea House Publishers
Philadelphia

Basic Domestic Pet Library

A Cat in the Family
Amphibians Today
Aquarium Beautiful
Choosing the Perfect Cat
Dog Obedience Training
Dogs: Selecting the Best Dog for You
Ferrets Today
Guppies Today
Hamsters Today
Housebreaking and Training Puppies
Iguanas in Your Home
Kingsnakes & Milk Snakes
Kittens Today
Lovebirds Today
Parakeets Today
Pot-bellied Pigs
Rabbits Today
Turtles Today

This edition © 1997 Chelsea House Publishers, a division of Main Line Book Company

© yearBOOKS, Inc.

1 3 5 7 9 8 6 4 2

Library of Congress Cataloging-in-Publication Data

Nieuwenhuizen, A. van den.
    Aquarium beautiful : a complete and up-to-date guide / A. van de
Nieuwenhuizen.
        p.   cm. -- (Basic domestic pet library)
    "Approved by the A.S.P.C.A."
    Includes index.
    ISBN 0-7910-4603-6 (hardcover)
    1. Aquariums. 2. Aquarium fishes. 3. Aquarium plants.
I. American Society for the Prevention of Cruelty to Animals.
II. Title. III. Series.
SF457.N53   1997
639.34--dc21   97-4187
                                                          CIP

The AQUARIUM BEAUTIFUL
by Arend van den Nieuwenhuizen

Photos by the author unless specifically credited otherwise

PREFACE

yearBOOK

yearBOOKS, INC.
Dr. Herbert R. Axelrod,
Founder & Chairman
Neal Pronek
Chief Editor

yearBOOKS are all photo composed, color separated, and designed on Scitex equipment in Neptune, N.J. with the following staff:

DIGITAL PRE-PRESS
Robert Onyrscuk
Jose Reyes
Michael L. Secord

COMPUTER ART
Sherise Buhagiar
Patti Escabi
Sandra Taylor Gale
Pat Marotta
Joanne Muzyka

ADVERTISING SALES
George Campbell
Chief
Amy Manning
Director

©yearBOOKS,Inc.
1 TFH Plaza
Neptune, N.J. 07753
Completely
manufactured in
Neptune, N.J.
USA

Arend van den Nieuwenhuizen is without a doubt one of the world's greatest natural history photographers. His photos have appeared in natural history books and magazines and he probably has more aquarium photos published than anyone else working in the field. Taking photos of aquarium fishes, both portraits and action shots of them spawning, requires a great deal of skill, patience and knowledge. You must know HOW the fish spawn so you can be ready to photograph the event when they do.

Since Arend is Dutch and the Dutch are famed for their magnificent aquariums, we suggested to Arend that he do this yearBOOK to give us some of the Dutch secrets.

He complied with our request and supplied us with a wonderful text and great photos showing various Dutch aquariums and how to set them up. I have taken the liberty of re-writing the text because although Arend's spoken English is excellent, his written English naturally needs refinement. Basically the ideas are his so I'll take responsibility for communicating his ideas.

Dr. Herbert R. Axelrod

You can have a beautiful Dutch aquarium, like this one, simply by following the instructions in this book.

CONTENTS

AN AQUARIUM WITH STYLE

By far, the majority of hobbyists are really *fish hobbyists* and not *aquarium hobbyists*. Usually the more advanced hobbyists breed aquarium fishes or even raise aquatic plants, but these are sidelines to the keeping of an aquarium with fishes. Some hobbyists specialize in specific groups of fishes like cichlids. Many cichlids chew up and destroy plants, so keeping cichlids in a beautiful aquarium is almost impossible. But even if the aquarist is crazy about fishes, he is also in love with a beautiful aquarium. You can see this behavior at fish shows. They spend a few minutes looking at a tank filled with angelfishes, but show them a magnificent Dutch aquarium and they will spend ten times as much of their leisure studying the layout, plants and how the fishes react within this beautiful underwater garden. Is there anyone who wouldn't like to have a beautiful Dutch aquarium in their living room? An aquarium that can serve as a night light, or as a living *bunch of plants*? No, my friends, there isn't a single fish hobbyist who wouldn't like to have a Dutch aquarium in the living room, but mother won't let them because they are not confident that the Dutch aquarium will actually be beautiful and become the centerpiece of the room. A Dutch aquarium features plants, not fishes. It cannot be designed or maintained by someone else. It is strictly personal; the creator must care for it, plan it, prune it and take pride in it. You can't start it and turn over the maintenance to junior.

WHAT IS A DUTCH AQUARIUM?

All over the world people speak about a *Dutch Aquarium*. They want to know how the Dutch can do it. Actually, though the Dutch started the Dutch aquarium beautifully the Japanese have almost overtaken them with their so-called *natural* aquariums. Most famous amongst the Japanese is Takashi Amano, the father of the Nature Aquarium concept. For more information, see his book *Nature Aquarium World*.

Aquarium:	200x40x40 cm.
Aquarium Furniture:	Framework covered with cork blocks.
Light hood:	7 cm. high, of dark painted wood. At the back in the cover of the light hood a strip of frosted glass (180x20) for indirect light in the room above the tank.
Distance:	floor to bottom of tank 50 cm.
Lighting:	at the left side front > back 1 Philips 'TL'D 36W/83 14 hours 1 Osram L 18W/Fluora 4 hours 1 Philips 'TL'D 32W/55 HF 6hours at the right side front > back 1 Philips 'TL'D 18W/83 14 hours 1 Osram L 36W/Floura 14 hours 1 Philips 'TL'D 16W/55 HF 6 hours
Decoration:	terraces of bogwood, Styropor-walls.
Equipment:	all equipment on the other side of the wall in another room in a chest.

But the Dutch do it without a lot of gadgets. So this book is how to make a beautiful Dutch aquarium with as few gadgets as possible. However, while many gadgets are not necessary, some are. Heaters, pumps, filters, lights, stands, canopies (covers for the tank) and a few other things like fertilizer, fish food, thermometers, water testers, and books, are all necessities. The high tech Japanese have many more gadgets, including those supplying carbon dioxide on demand, adjusting the lights to simulate morning, evening light gradients, etc.

But the task of this book is to enable you to have a Dutch aquarium as inexpensively as possible...for the Dutch are also famous for their thrift!

Remember this: An aquarium is a living microcosm. All the gadgets in the world can't help you keep the plants and fishes alive unless you know the needs of the plants and fishes and how to use the gadgets properly. If you know how to keep the plants and fishes alive without gadgets, then buying them is a labor-saving technique and not a necessity.

So, what you will read as you move on through this book are general principles on how to make a beautiful aquarium, both inside and outside. There are tips, tricks and directions based upon actual experiences. The aquariums have not been set up for this book, they are all living, well established Dutch tanks that serve as models upon which you can design your own Dutch aquarium.

WHERE TO LOCATE YOUR DUTCH AQUARIUM

Many aquarists (and books!) don't really tackle the question of where to locate the aquarium. They talk about windows, radiators, doorways and traffic. Be careful! The location of the aquarium can determine in advance whether your Dutch aquarium will be a boom or a bust!

There are very few locations in any given room that are suitable for an aquarium. The major concern is light! It is much easier to control the light if you supply 99% of it through artificial means, using fluorescent tubes or more powerful lamps which may be used for highlighting or for supplying a particular area of the tank with more light than the rest of the tank requires.

The first idea to get out of your head is that natural light is good enough for a Dutch aquarium. This is just not true! In the temperate zones, where most of our readers live, the direction from which sunlight enters our windows changes. The sun rises in the east and sets in the west, so the morning light comes in the eastern window(s) and the evening sun comes through the western window(s). Unfortunately, the angle changes, too, so in the summer the sun's rays come straight down, giving us more heat than in the winter, when they are at an angle and give us much less heat (thus causing summer and winter). Not only does the outside air temperature change with the seasons, thanks to Earth's movements, but those same movements also dictate the *length of the day*. Usually the

Aquarium:	160x50x50 cm.
Aquarium Furniture:	the tank stands on a table
Distance:	floor to bottom of tank 40 cm.
Light hood:	4.5 cm. high. Synthetic material
Lighting in the past:	1 Philips TL 65W/32
	1 Sylvania TL 65W/GroLux
Lighting:	2 bulbs each 5W
later:	1 Philips 'TL'D 58W/83
front:	1 Sylvania TL 65/WGroLux
back:	2 bulbs each 5W
Decoration:	bottom flat, no terraces

A very beautiful example of a big tank that stands only 30 cm above the floor. The fishes in this tank are not shy because the decoration inside is built up with hiding places, and "sun and shadow." In the light-cover is a 10 cm glass strip for indirect lighting and to give access to feed for the fishes.

longest day of the year (in the Northern Hemisphere) is around the third week of June when northern Europe may have 20 hours of daylight! And in December they have shorter days, with 20 hours of darkness. Obviously, the sun is the aquarium's enemy. The sun can cook the fish or turn the water pea-soup green from being too bright and too strong.

So, where is the best place to locate your aquarium? In the darkest corner of the living room where it gets little, if any, sunlight! We will control the light so that it is on for 12 hours a day, the way it is around the equator where many of the fishes and plants thrive.

There are many advantages to controlling the light in an aquarium, as some plants require much less light *(Cryptocoryne)* than do such fast growing plants as *Anacharis* or *Cabomba.*

WHAT SIZE AQUARIUM?

There is no question that *the bigger the better.* The larger aquarium allows you to isolate patches of light, maintain more balanced water temperatures, make plants more contrasting as far as size is concerned, and, generally speaking, caring for a larger aquarium is easier than for a smaller one (within reason). But keep in mind that the larger the tank, the more everything will cost, including the water plants.

Most aquarium shops sell tanks by their capacity. Most of these designations are slightly incorrect and can be very misleading. Our guide to selecting the proper size is:

Get the largest size you can easily afford, and be sure your floor can sustain the weight. Water weighs 8.25 pounds per gallon, or l kg per liter. A 100 gallon aquarium, with its substrate and other gadgets, might reach 1000 pounds! Can your floor handle it?

To temper the suggestion that you get the tallest affordable tank, keep in mind that the tank must be twice as long as the depth and height. The depth and height should be about équal. An 18" x 18" x 30" tank is a good start. In general, a deeper tank is better than a shallow tank of the same water capacity, even though the interface with the atmosphere is better with a shallow tank. That's why we often use a pump and filter.

Angelfish tanks, which are very deep and fairly narrow, are not good for decorating purposes. Imagine how you would clean a tank 48 inches deep? Stick with the 18" x 18" x 30" tank. It is usually a standard size and is not too expensive when compared to less desirable sizes.

Of course you have to consider the space available in your living room. If you don't have a footprint of 18" x 30", it might be necessary to have a tank built to your

There is no question that "the bigger the better." The larger aquarium allows you to isolate patches of light.

The supporting lip for this tank is bolted to the wall, and the single supporting leg has been placed at the center of gravity. The leg has been shimmed at its bottom to provide 100% levelness to the tank.

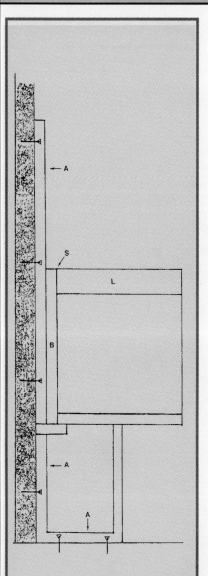

Construction to bear an aquarium on a framework which extends back. Iron framework is 5 cm, welded together.

A. Supports and beams bolted into the wall and screwed into the floor.
B. Airduct between the aquarium and the wall.
L. Lighting hood.
S. Hinge of the lighting hood.

specifications (keep the proportion in mind of 2:1:1) or, failing that, you might even try to build your own tank (recommended only for people handy with tools and with no one living underneath them!).

WHAT COMES WITH THE TANK?

Most aquariums today are made of glass which is glued together with a silicone-based cement. They have no frames and they usually are sold without hoods (canopies), lamps or stands. To be a true work of art, you must have a suitable source of light. The lights are usually located in the hood. You want the hood with the least height,

(sand, gravel, etc.), filters, suitable tank backgrounds, if you want to hide the sides and back, and the best lamps for the hood. Some things that might come with the tank are leaks, explosions (a glass breaks under pressure), or cave-ins where the downstairs neighbors get a shower from their ceiling. You also might blow fuses, have the tanks used for dumping alcoholic drinks or as an ashtray, if your life style includes such parties...but in general, once you've had an engineer give you his opinion about the floor and the electrical hazards, everything should easily be controlled.

"Make sure the guarantee comes from the manufacturer..."

preferably made of stainless steel. You want a low height, so the lamps are close to the surface of the water. Since tanks are usually located against a wall or in a corner, the back of the tank will eventually be covered. But suppose you want to use the tank as a room divider? Or to fit into a remote corner? Then we need a triangular tank, something like a prism. Finding a suitable hood for such a tank could be impossible. So be careful with the aquarium you build or order...it may not have a hood which fits it. Without a suitable hood you cannot have a Dutch aquarium. It's that simple. You simply must be able to control the light.

Things that should come with your tank are heaters, thermometers, substrate

Obviously, one of the most important things that comes with an aquarium is a guarantee.

Make sure it is in writing and signed. You probably will need an invoice to prove where you bought the tank. Never buy a used tank from anyone. Start out with a new tank that has been tested (by you) for leaks. This is especially true of uncommon sizes.

Since leaks are not uncommon from dripping arms, nets and jumping fishes, you should not place your tank on top of anything electrical, especially your stereo, computer or television set. In any case, having the Dutch aquarium as an isolated thing of beauty is more important than having it compete with your stereo or TV set.

This is an example of a tank which divides one part of the room from the other. It is also an example of a tank where you can look on the water surface from above.

WHAT YOU NEED TO SUPPORT THE TANK

To support your aquarium you need money (no joke!) to enable you to buy exactly what you want and to outfit it properly. Since the Dutch aquarium is a dream tank, don't settle for anything less than ideal for you and the space you have available.

Aquarium:	**200x50x50 (Juwel-aquarium)**
Light hood:	**5 cm high**
Lighting:	
past:	**1 Philips TL 65W/32**
	1 Philips TL 65W/33
	2 Philips TL 8W/33
later:	**1 Philips 'TL'D 58W/83 (12 hours)**
	1 Philips 'TL'D 58W/84 (9 hours)
	2 Philips TL 8W/ 33 (12 hours)
Decoration:	**bogwood between the plants, highest terrace 15 cm. Walls of Styropor, painted in several natural colors, partially grown over with *Vesicularia dubyana*.**
Filter:	**change water every week 20% fresh water.**

Wait, if necessary, until you have enough money to get started. You don't have to buy *everything* at once, but you do have to start with the basics. The first thing you need is not the aquarium. It is that which supports the aquarium..**the aquarium stand**.

In Holland, it is not unusual for the aquarist to build his own aquarium. This is NOT true at all in the English-speaking world. So your first

Above: A tank of 150x50x50 cm on an iron frame with a chest. Below: The same tank a year after installation, re-fitted into a supporting stand and framed in plywood. The chest at the lower right side contains the filter and the lighting timers.

task is to decide on the tank you need and then decide upon its support.

Tanks are traditionally supported on an aquarium stand. This is a heavy steel or iron frame with four legs, a top shelf and usually a shelf about a foot off the ground, which holds the stand together at the bottom (prevents the legs from spreading apart) and which might be able to support another aquarium slightly smaller than the one on top. Assuming you know the size of the bottom of your ideal aquarium, check the ability of the floor to carry the potential weight and acquire the stand. Most stands for aquariums are not things of beauty, so you might want to coat it with paint, formica or to hide it within a cabinet. Of course, there are more sophisticated stands already made as parts of a cabinet. The cabinet has many advantages, the best being that it looks like a piece of furniture already, that can be used to hold/hide foods, fertilizers and electrical outlets (for the heater, pumps, etc.), and muffles the sound of the pump.

The latest of styles in Holland is what we call the *hanging aquarium*. This is an aquarium fastened to the wall without the need of an aquarium stand. This would be acceptable for tanks smaller than 36" x 18" x 18" but you have to work with an engineer to be sure the wall is strong

enough and the bolts long enough, and that it is safe from collapsing the whole wall or floor. Some very long and slightly high tanks, with little depth from the front glass to

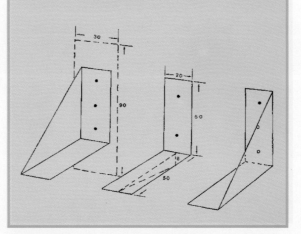

Supports used for the hanging aquarium. The dotted lines indicate the five-millimeter-thick iron supports on the other side of the wall.

the wall, might work.

Of course you can always support the hanging aquarium by putting two legs under the tank to support it. I have taken two photos. One shows the tank hanging, while the

other shows the same tank in the same room, but this time on a four-legged stand. The frame around the tank is hand-made, constructed of plywood. The hanging aquarium shown here is supported by two heavy steel plates that are fastened to the outside of the wall (outside the house). The plates measure about 35 inches long and 8 inches wide. They are about one fifth of an inch (5 mm) thick and can stand the weight of a metric ton (2200 pounds). The tank supports and the steel plates go right through the wall. This sort of arrangement is only good when the wall is an outside wall made of strong wood. It doesn't work too well if the wall is made of brick unless you want to have a major construction job! Don't even think about it if your walls are hollow and covered with plasterboard. In any case, such construction requires the approval of an architect or engineer. *The decision to make a hanging aquarium should not be guess-work.*

The Dutch rule is to isolate and insulate your aquarium. You want to protect everything around the tank from moisture which will evaporate, and from the heat. The tank is usually hotter than the air around it, thus you want to insulate all the sides, and top and bottom, which are not utilized for viewing the inside of the tank.

The bottom of the tank is

Aquarium:	140x50x50 cm
Aquarium Furniture:	140x57 including light hood. The self-made tank and the piece of furniture under the tank form a whole (length 180 cm). Drawers and chest of synthetic material.
Light hood:	7 cm high, made of synthetic material.
Distance:	floor to bottom of tank 70 cm.
Lighting:	1 Philips 'TL'D 32W HF/83
	1 Osram L 40W/Floura
	1 Philips 'TL'D 32W HF/83
	1 Philips 'TL'D 36W/82
	4 bulbs of 40 watts each in combination with a dimmer for "sundown" and "sunrise."
Decoration:	Small terraces for natural stones.
Equipment:	In the chest at the right side.

easily insulated and isolated (to dampen the noise) by placing it on anything strong and relatively soft. You can use a piece of thick carpet, a piece of styrofoam, a flat piece of soft balsa wood, or even an old ceiling tile. The frame of the tank (including the hood) is usually covered with wood and stained to match the furniture in the room. Most Dutch hobbyists use plywood and then glue veneer onto the plywood so it matches the furniture.

While locating the tank in the living room you have already kept it from the sun's rays. Now keep in mind that you want to be able to sit and stare at it while you relax. That's what the Dutch aquarium is all about.

This is a half-hanging tank. Behind the strip there are amplifiers fitted as bottom heaters. Because the weight bearers are flat it was necessary to use two supports at the left and right sides under the tank. It is a pity that one can see the socket right under the tank and the electric wires at the left side.

A half-hanging aquarium with the furnishing of the tank as a good contrast to the wall and the chest that is under the tank, with both having the same covering.

This is an aquarium from Germany. The basis for this tank is the description of Dutch tanks. The furnishing is very beautiful and formed as a wall chest, but above the tank there is no chest but only a wooden front, which revolves. In this way it is possible to work in the tank. At the left side there is a door; there is also one at the right side. This is where the hobbyist can go behind the tank. Behind the back side of the tank is the house wall. Under the tank is a real chest with a biological filter on both sides. The principle occupiers are *Pterophyllum scalare* together with tetras like *Hyphessobrycon erythrostigma.*

THE SCIENCE OF AQUARIUM DECORATION

THE GOLDEN INTERSECTION.

You cannot have a Dutch aquarium without a design in mind BEFORE you set up your aquarium. You simply cannot set up the aquarium and randomly place the stones, rocks, substrata, plants and fish without an exact idea of what you are doing. It's not that there aren't many tanks simply organized in this manner. The plants are healthy and growing, the fish are thriving, but the tank lacks that special beauty that only a clever Dutch design can generate.

We need a tank in which the plants will be placed according to our wishes. There is no sense in planting tall plants in front of short ones...you'll never see the shorter ones! You need to arrange the dark green plants as backgrounds to the light green ones; the bushy plants should contrast with the leafy ones. The only way for beginners to do this is by making a sketch. Throughout this book are illustrations of sketches made before the planting. Because this is a book, the sketches were made by an aquatic artist who knows about Dutch aquariums and aquarium plants. The special effect of a Dutch tank is that it is terraced. The plants get taller and taller as they recede from the front (viewing) glass. In each Dutch aquarium there is a main theme. If you are an amateur photographer or painter, you will know that the

eye goes immediately to the strong point of the art piece. This strong point is located according to the golden intersection.

DRAWING THE GOLDEN INTERSECTION

Draw the base of an aquarium which is 18" x 36", or, even more likely a Dutch tank would be 60 x 150 cm (24 x 60 inches). We require a straight-edge and a compass. The right hand panel of the tank is represented by the line BC. We extend this line by half of the length of the front panel line which we call $^1/_2$B. The end of the line, Z, is joined to A. Using a compass measure the length ZB and scribe a partial circle from point B to the intersection which we denote as Y. Then at point A, measure AY, and mark the intersection of this arc with AB and we denote it as point 2 on the front pane.

We do exactly the same things with the left hand side of the aquarium where the line CD is lengthened by $^1/_2$ of DA. Making the arc, we call it point 4. From point 2 a line is drawn from the front to the back pane, and from point 4 a line connects (dotted line) the two side panels. The intersection of these two lines at point 5 is called the **strong point.** The lines are called **strong lines**. Using this same technique three more strong points can be discovered. The **strong points** are at the intersections of all the inside

lines plus a homologous point. This is the technique of the **golden intersection**.

Using the Strong Points

In connection with the view direction (you usually look at the tank from the front, through the largest pane), the terraces and plant groups are located according to the strong points. If this sounds complicated at this stage, study the various planted aquaria and it will become much clearer. In most tanks only one or two strong points are used. One strong point is usually a large, solitary plant like an Amazon Swordplant. The other is a large rock which may be half hidden by suitable plants around it. The accompanying drawing is

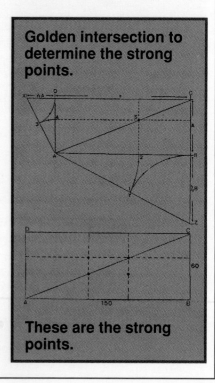

Golden intersection to determine the strong points.

These are the strong points.

helpful in understanding this concept. Actually, the larger the tank, the more strong points can be utilized. For the 160 cm (6") tank, all four strong points can be utilized to highlight the decor.

Each strong point can be an eye catcher. The front strong points can use a thick solitary plant that isn't too tall, while the rear strong points use solitary plants, which are much taller than the forward strong points. Only use plants that grow straight up for strong points. We don't want these plants to grow sideways!

A favorite for the sides of the Dutch tank is the inexpensive rooted plant called Corkscrew Val (try *Vallisneria americana, V. gigantea, V. spiralis*). The groups of *Vallisneria* should not be equal. Put 35% more in the right hand side. Then a huge, beautiful *Aponogeton ulvaceus*, or another *Aponogeton* species, can be planted by itself on the right side. Large plants can be located at the strong points. They can be the same species or plants within the same genus, or they can be similar plants in a different genus. Study the illustrations and characteristics of the various plants illustrated in this book and then visit your local fish store and see what they have in stock or what they can order for you. *Tropical Fish Hobbyist* magazine always carries advertisements from growers selling fancy plants, but it's easier to buy them from your local pet shop operator.

BUILDING A TERRACE

Terraces are built according to the viewing angle. Let's

Example of the construction plan for an aquarium 160x60x60 centimeters with the possibilities of different view directions and the adapted organization as far as depth perception is concerned. Two strong points are used. In addition, a complete coconut shell is placed at point C as a possible spawning spot for dwarf cichlids; at points B and D half coconut shells are buried in the bottom for the same purpose, and more possibilities are created at point A for the same reason. The numbers relate to the heights of the terraces.

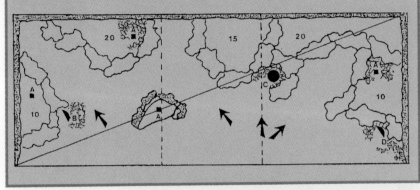

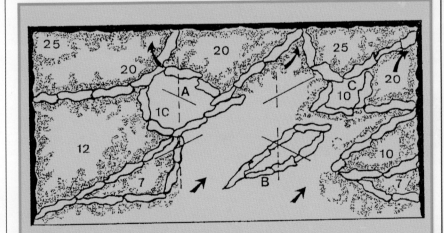

Here the assumed direction of view goes from left in front to the right (straight arrow). The curved arrows indicate the spots where we can strengthen the depth effect with "look-throughs" between the plants. Points A and B are strong points, where at B the depth effect is even strengthened by a few flat stones in the view direction and also by a group of low growing plants. We could place a tall growing solitary plant, a beautiful *Echinodorous,* at the shifted strong point C. This *Echinodorous* will even emphasize the space behind. The numbers correspond to the height of the terraces when the height of the tank is 60 cms(24").

In this aquarium a beautiful group of *Echinodorus* stays only 10 cms (4") behind the front pane. This is possible because there is not only a view from the front, but you can look in the tank from left to right and from right to left. Furthermore, a big piece of bogwood lays from the left hand pane to the bottom to the right hand pane up to the water surface. So it is possible to provide a shadow and hiding places for fishes like *Pareutropics buffei* or *Synodontis nigriventris.*

consider a tank that is in the center of the room, but the couch is on the left, so the aquarium will be viewed from the center left. This means we will have a strongly planted left front and a thinly planted right rear. The sketch shows this very clearly. You can also consider planting large solitary plants (*Aponogeton*) at the strong points marked A,B and C. The terraces are accentuated by the strong points.

All the terraces in the front of the aquarium are low,

below 3 inches in overall height, while the rear can rise to 10 inches. This enables us to build a solid wall of plants in the back. At strong point B, a flat terrace is built. Use lava stones or flat stones that are about an inch thick, which should be clumped so that they form an interesting centerpiece. Of course, it must be low since it is in the front of the aquarium!

We shall use the low and slow growing *Cryptocoryne willisii* (which is the same as *nevillii*) or some other plants

like *Proserpinaca pectinata* or *Heteranthera zosterifolia*. At point C we need a large plant like *Aponogeton ulvaceus* to contrast with the *Echinodorus cordifolius*. You need large plants that should have large leaves of different shapes.

In order to have the plants not competing with each other and looking alike, we never use large solitary plants in the front of the aquarium; nor do we put it in the middle, where it can be called a *centerpiece*. Centerpieces become boring after a while because your eye always travels to it.

One inventive aquarist decided to construct an aquarium with the front glass slanted from right to left. In other words, the left hand panel is more narrow than the right hand panel. This gives us an interesting perspective with which to work.

The slanted front removes glare and caters to someone who would view the tank from the left side (sitting on the couch). With proper planting, this tank can have a huge apparent depth. But care must be taken that when the aquarium is viewed from the front, it doesn't look badly. Thus we have a problem of adorning an aquarium that has to be interesting when viewed from the front and from the left. The accompanying illustration shows how this was done.

The large plants need not always be in the rear, nor should the short plants always be in the foreground. A group of tall-growing plants, like *Vallisneria*, in the front can be interesting from both the front and side views. The Val grows upwards and eventually the leaves float.

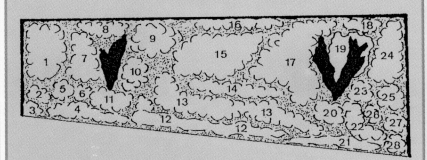

1. *Hygrophila difformis*
2. *Myriophyllum matogrossense*
3. *Hydrocotyle leucoaetala*
4. *Echinodorus quadricostatus (magdalensis)*
5. *Marsilea crenata*
6. *Eleocharis acicularis*
7. *Alternanthera reineckii ("rosaefolia")*
8. *Myriophyllum scabratum*
9. *Echinodorus osiris*
10. *Bacopa caroliniana*
11. *Nymphaea lotus* (green, spotted)
12. *Vesicularia dubyana*
13. *Cryptocoryne wendtii*
14. *Cryptocoryne willisii*
15. *Alternanthera reineckii ("rosefolia")*
16. *Vallisneria spiralis*
17. *Lobelia cardinalis*
18. *Ludwigia repens x palustris*
19. *Myriophyllum aquaticum*
20. *Eichhornea azurea*
21. *Heteranthera zosterifolia*
22. *Saururus cornutus*
23. *Cryptocoryne balansae (=crispatula)*
24. *Hygrophila corymbosa*
25. *Acorus gramineus*
26. *Rotala macrantha*
27. *Myriophyllum matogrossense*
28. *Vallisneria americana (=gigantea)*

Bogwood used as an open hiding place.
KW=Cork wall with hole in which the wood is fastened.
Plants: *Microsorium pteropus, Anubias barteri var.nana* and *Vesicularia dubyana.*

The same piece of wood used only as decoration.
A= screw through the perspex bottom plate
B= vertical glued strips of perspex used as supports
C= left open hole in the wood for a group of small plants or just one as *Cardimine lyrata*
D= left open hole in the wood for a decorative smaller or bigger plant, for instance *Scripus, Vallisneria* or *Echinodorus.*

This is interesting.

The dark background of this setup allows for almost picture perfection from several viewing angles. The dark background also highlights the fishes, especially if you have light-colored (Cardinal Tetras, for example) or silvery fishes (hatchetfishes, for example).

The *golden intersection* is not a law! It is actually a principle by which skillful artists and photographers work. It is NOT the only way to lay out an aquarium. Think of the many ways flowers can be arranged in a vase; well aquariums can be decorated the same way. The flowers can be loose, informal and

Looking at the aquarium from the right in front to the left, as shown in the picture, you see how the depth in the decoration of this aquarium is lost.

friendly, requiring much less maintenance, or they can be formal and rigid, requiring constant pruning to keep plant levels (heights and density) in their proper perspective. At many aquarium exhibitions you will see mostly informal aquariums set ups, which are quite beautiful, but they almost always lack depth! And the main reason for the lack of depth is that there are too many plants. Such aquaria are better called *underwater gardens*. They are beautiful but become overgrown unless carefully planted, as most plants grow at differing rates.

As a general rule, plants clumped in bunches must always be as far from the viewing point as possible. They should always have lots of room because bunch plants (as they are called in the trade) grow very quickly (if they grow at all). If they merely survive, they usually become stringy and ugly and shed leaves. It takes an extremely skillful aquarist to decorate his aquarium with bunch plants (like *Anacharis, Cabomba,* and *Elodea*). The slow growing plants are by far the best. Just get smaller sizes of the *Anubias, Aponogeton,* etc.

SMALL AQUARIUMS

For the sake of the fishes and plants, the larger the aquarium, the better for the inhabitants. However, not everyone has the resources (money, space) for a large aquarium. There is no limit on the size of any aquarium (within reason). If an aquarium is too deep, then the light will not be able to penetrate into the depths to achieve photosynthesis in the plants at the bottom of the tank. Using very strong lights would only create algae in the upper reaches of the tank. So we need high terracing in a deep tank, with stones, roots and other decorations for the bottom. The high terracing brings the plants within the effective range of the lights.

So, for small or large deep tanks we require more skills than for the recommended 18" x 18" x 30" size. A tank with 10" (25 cm) height is very difficult to plant beautifully...but it can be successfully decorated with fewer plants using driftwood and cork.

DRIFTWOOD

A natural look is simple. Go out into your local small stream or ditch and look at the old decaying branches, trees and trunks *decorating* this dismal view. *DON'T TAKE ANY OF THESE FOR YOUR AQUARIUM AS THEY ARE ALMOST SURELY POISONED WITH HEAVY METALS OR PESTICIDES!* Your local pet shop has plenty of driftwood in many sizes and shapes. The size you want depends, of course, on the size of your aquarium. Your aquarium must be designed around the driftwood. Using a huge piece

of driftwood, you can make an embankment with the sand being held back by the driftwood. In this case, as in most cases, the driftwood must be fastened to a base. The usual base is a piece of cement in which the driftwood is placed prior to its hardening. If you make this base yourself, be careful. The cement must be properly treated (soaking it in vinegar and then painting it with a double coating of waterproof varnish) or it will cause water chemistry problems due to the alkali it releases.

It is also possible to use a cork wall in the aquarium and to imbed the branches of the driftwood into this background. It is very attractive but difficult to live with. The main problem is catching a fish in a tank decorated with driftwood. The driftwood cannot be moved and the net invariably gets tangled in it. So, as usual, you trade beauty for convenience.

CORK

Real or artificial cork is

usually available either from your local pet shop or from your local hardware store. It comes in tiles of about 10" (25 cm) square and about ¼" (6 mm) thick.

The cork can usually be glued to the back and, perhaps, the sides, of the aquarium using silastic aquarium glue. It takes very little glue to make the cork adhere to the glass. Use as little glue as possible because it will be very difficult to remove the cork, should you ever decide to remove it. The cork must also be firmly attached so the edges do not warp and allow debris to settle in inaccessible areas. This might cause a pollution problem. There are many ways to solve this problem.

The easiest solution is to glue the cork tiles onto a sheet of safe, non-water soluble plastic. The plastic does not even have to be rigid. It can be of slightly smaller dimensions than the back glass of the tank and it can be prepared outside the tank on a flat table or floor surface. You can

The same tank as on the facing page, shown in a frontal view; notice how the high terracing in a deep tank, with stones, roots, and other decorations for the bottom, brings the plants within the effective range of the lights.

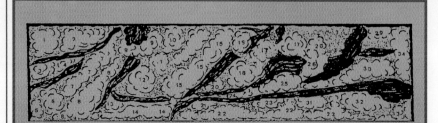

1. *Hygrophila corymbosa*
2. *Rotala macrantha*
3. *Myriophyllum scabratum*
4. *Marsilea crenata*
5. *Ceratophyllum demersum*
6. *Echinodorus horizontalis*
7. *Eleocharis acicularis*
8. *Proserpinaca pectinata (Hottonia inflata)*
9. *Didiplis diandra*
10. *Hygrophyla corymbosa*
11. *Cryptocoryne beckettii*
12. *Nymphaea lotus* (red-brown)
13. *Eichhornia azurea*
14. *Eleocharis parvula*
15. *Blyxa aubertii* var. *echinosperma*
16. *Limnophila aquatica*
17. *Cryptocoryne balansae (crispatula)*
18. *Echinodorus opacus*
19. *Ammania gracilis*
20. *Nuphar sagittifolium*
21. *Eichhornia natans*
22. *Echinodorus tenellus*
23. *Rotala wallichii*
24. *Saururus cernuus*
25. *Nympheae lotus* (green, spotted)
26. *Myriophyllum aquaticum*
27. *Microsorium pteropus*
28. *Rotala rotundifolia*
29. *Vesicularia dubyana* (at the walls)
30. *Cryptocoryne undulata*
31. *Heteranthera zosterifolia*
32. *Saururus cernuus*
33. *Cryptocoryne undulata*
34. *Vallisneria asiatica* var. *biwaensis* (syn. *V. spiralis* forma *tortifolia*)

use as much silastic as you need. Once this background is glued in position, it should be allowed to set for a day or two, then soaked with a hose to remove the residue of the silastic (it smells like vinegar) and to remove small particles of cork that might clog your filter. The additional beauty of making the cork background on glass or plastic is that you can build your own flowerpots out of pieces of cork tile. These flowerpots can be glued onto the cork wall and you then can have short plants (like *Cryptocoryne*) growing at differing heights adding very effective variety to your decor. Because most *Cryptocoryne* are slow growing, their positioning needn't change for a long time. As a matter of fact, a very interesting way to use these flowerpots is to plant the *Cryptocoryne*, or any similar bog plant, with its leaves lying on the surface of the water. Such plants will almost surely begin to grow out of the water and, because they are so close to the light, might even blossom! The plants that can be used successfully with this technique are *Cryptocoryne willisii* (=*C. nevillii*), *C. beckettii*, *Echinodorus tenellus*, *Hydrocotyle vulgaris*, just to name a few.

A very effective use of the cork background is to use the flowerpots to plant Java Moss (*Vesicularia dubyana*). It might eventually cover the entire cork background with lush green leaves.

Some lumber yards are even able to supply real cork bark, or even cut branches which have the cork bark on the branches (it doesn't even have to be real cork!). You can

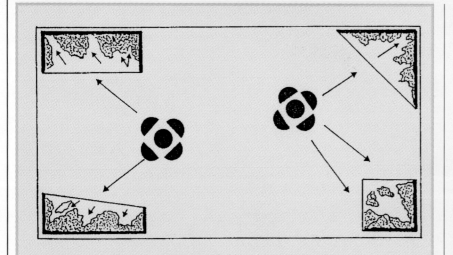

Settee-combination with several view-directions in connection with the depth in the decoration of an aquarium somewhere in the living room.

are three excellent reasons for not attaching the cork, or anything like cork, to the back of the tank:

1. If the glass breaks for any reason, especially when you are working on it, everything will be wasted. If the tank is set up, you will have a flood, dead fish and a mess on your hands!
2. Changing the walls is almost impossible.
   3. If the aquarium is taken out of service for a while (moving, illness, lack of space because the new baby needs the room), the cork or bark will usually dry out and warp, making it unusable because of

cut the branches so that you have about one quarter of the circumference on small planks. These then can be glued together or attached to a piece of plastic, glass or even waterproof plywood. Again, flowerpots can be made from the same bark and generally the use is the same as the cork tiles, but the cork tiles are MUCH easier to work with...and are much safer. Some trees are unsuitable for aquarium purposes. Check with your dealer.

If you have ANY doubt about the safety of cork, bark or anything else that you want to put into your tank, simply boil it in water. Allow the water to cool to aquarium temperature and then put into this water some sensitive fishes like Guppies, Platies, Swordtails or Mollies. If the fish die, you know the answer! Allow the fish to live in the test water for a week before you draw any conclusions.

WARNING: *It is not wise to attach anything to the aquarium glass itself.* There

This picture illustrates the use of a solitary plant on bogwood to add to the decoration of the aquarium.

The same tank as on page 24, but shown from a slightly different angle to illustrate the effect that angulation can have on the viewer's perception of depth.

the spaces created for debris.

PROCESSING THE CORK OR BARK

Once the choice has been made and the cork or bark is glued onto a background, it must be soaked. Of course you could also soak it before you use it, but cork tiles will warp into unusable shapes if you try this. So take the

mounted cork or bark and soak it in a running stream. Of course we don't expect everyone reading this book to have a stream in his back yard, so soak the background in anything available, like a bathtub. If you only have a very small bathtub but a large aquarium, make the background in smaller pieces which you can then glue

together using a strip of plastic to hold the pieces. These smaller pieces can be soaked more easily.

Also, if you are just setting up the tank, use the tank to soak the background. This cleans the tank as well as the background. The sand may also be cleaned in this manner.

To soak the cork or bark merely use water as hot (or warm) as is easily attainable. Keep soaking the bark and cork until the water turns brown. Then change the water. Keep doing this until the water stays clear after 3 days of constant soaking. The whole process may take up to two weeks. In some cases it is possible to use the brown water, but check the pH. If the pH is too low (meaning its acid), say, below pH 6.0, then don't use the water. Cardinal Tetras and other Rio Negro fishes do well in this tannic acid water. Most cichlid and livebearers do poorly (except the Discus that come from the Rio Negro, all of which are *Symphysodon discus* varieties).

It is often possible and desirable to glue some cork or bark onto a piece of slate or glass and use this to form a terrace. If you are very handy, you can get some plastic that softens in hot water and then it can be formed to fit the area you wish to be terraced. The curves of the warped plastic is then covered with cork tile and it becomes very decorative.

The cork tiles, by the way, fade in direct sunlight. Not all cork is safe for the aquarium. It must all be tested by the soaking method described above.

In some cases it is possible to use the brown water, but check the pH. Test kits like these make pH testing simple. Photo compliments of Wardley.

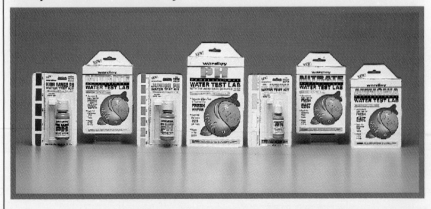

Most cichlids and livebearers, except those that come from the Rio Negro, such as this *Symphysodon discus* variety, do poorly in acidic conditions.

PLANTS...THE FINISHING TOUCH IN CREATING A DUTCH AQUARIUM

Are plants the finishing touch...or are they the beginning? If you have made up your mind to have a Dutch aquarium, then plants had to be the basis of the inspiration, because living plants are what the Dutch aquarium is all about. A Dutch aquarium is an underwater garden, though a few plants may be allowed to grow out from the aquarium's surface and penetrate the atmosphere with its leaves and flowers. Also, some

> ***"...the goal of a Dutch aquarium is to achieve a great visual depth."***

terrestrial plants may be positioned so that their adventitious roots may actually enter the aquarium. It is the natural tendency of rooted plants for their roots to seek water and they grow in the direction of the source of water.

As a general rule, pet shops that specialize in aquariums also carry live plants. The best plants are usually those that are grown in small plastic pots and you have the ability to buy them in a rooted condition. These plants have usually been grown under hydroponic conditions, where the food is liquid. When you get the plant home you should remove the pot but keep the roots imbedded in the ball of glass wool (or whatever the base medium is) and plant the entire ball and roots together. You can also keep them in the plastic pot, but then their growth is severely restricted. But this restriction of growth may be desirable in some cases.

To state the case simply, the goal of a Dutch aquarium is to achieve a great visual depth. This is also the case in many paintings and photographs. How to depict a three dimensional view in two dimensions (drawings, paintings, etc.) has been achieved by famous artists throughout history. Since few

You want to show a strong foreground.

of us are landscape geniuses, we have to rely upon the general principles of the golden intersection in order to achieve our goals of depth perception.

There are many plants suitable for the aquarium. Many, if not most, are bog plants and live better out of the water than they do submerged. It is even possible to use land plants for certain purposes, but you must realize that such plants ultimately die and can cause pollution havoc in the aquarium.

It is very difficult to write about what is *best* in an aquarium design. Every person has their own ideas of what is *best* for them. Remember Shakespeare's famous words *Beauty lies in the eyes of the beholder.* This is also true for putting together a Dutch aquarium. Thus, what follows are merely suggestions based upon more than 100 years of experience (Axelrod and van den Nieuwenhuizen have each kept Dutch aquariums for more than 50 years!). Make your own design. If you are satisfied, then by all means leave it alone and be happy. If you want to be more certain of success, then copy one of the designs illustrated in this book.

THE EFFECT OF PLANTS ON AQUARIUM FOREGROUNDS

You cannot achieve a depth and space perception without selecting those plants that will do best at a given spot in the aquarium. This book will not deal with every species of plant suitable for the aquarium. There are other, more complete books on that

In effect you want to reduce the visual size.

subject. But NO other book discusses those plants that live best together under a given set of circumstances. Certain small, low plants do best when NOT sheltered by the shade of a large, taller leafy plant. Aquarium plant books don't talk about this subject. They only discuss the identification, care and propagation of plants, perhaps with their origin and habitat. So keep in mind that there is more than one way to *skin a cat.* Our suggestions here are not laws...only suggestions. In all cases, try to make a sketch of the layout of your tank. Use the photos in this book, or in any book or magazine that shows the type of planted aquarium which appeals to you.

When starting to create an aquarium FOR EFFECT, we don't even think about the fish. Our desire is for an underwater garden. The fish can come later (if at all!). Interestingly enough, the successful Dutch water gardeners start from the front edge of the tank. In order to start properly you must keep in mind that the gravel depth line should NOT be visible from the front of the aquarium. The gravel (substrate) must slope from the back to the front in such a manner that it is almost non-existent when the substrate touches the front glass. There are two reasons for this: first, a gravel line visible from the front glass destroys the depth effect. Secondly, it doesn't

Make all of the front glass a pleasure to look at.

look good, and whatever amount of substrate showing on the front glass does, in effect, reduce the visual size of the aquarium. Imagine walking along a mountain pass. You see a magnificent peak and you want to photograph it. You take out your camera and focus when all of a sudden you see that the lower part of the peak is obstructed by the guard rail (to keep people from falling down the mountain). This unnatural obstruction of your view is what a substrate line does to the critical observer. There is another obvious example. When most inexperienced people take photographs of other people, they almost always use the other person's face to be the center of the photo. This results in the legs being cut off while the space above the head is usually uninteresting.

Make all of the front glass a pleasure to look at! In most cases, though, there must be some depth to the substrate at the front of the tank. In this case, a false frame is added to the base of the tank. This can be a piece of metal or some solid color paper glued to the base of the glass (on the outside of course). The false frame should always be at exactly the same height as the level of the gravel or substrate.

Just fixing the substrate height at the front glass can frequently be insufficient. If you insert the wrong plants at the front glass, plants that grow too wide or too bushy, then you have hidden too much of the interior of the tank and lost depth and space perception.

ECHINODORUS QUADRICOSTATUS

One of the plants that many

people recommend for the foreground is *Echinodorus quadricostatus* var. *xinguensis*. This plant easily and quickly reaches 10 cm (= 4 inches). When it grows well it reproduces by runners and soon blankets the bottom of the tank. A 4-inch tall blanket is too high. Your own lawn would not look well if it were too tall either! Starting with a foreground of 4 inches gives you a loss of depth perception for your slope to the background. You want the lowest growing plant possible for the foreground, that's why good Dutch aquarium farmers are very careful.

SAURURUS CERNUUS

Many aquarium designers use *Saururus cernuus* for their foreground plant. **WRONG!** While this is a very lovely plant it may require a lot of work. If used in the foreground, the plants must be changed to smaller plants every few weeks, depending upon the growth rate. This is most easily done by having a special swamp tank or plant aquarium with strong light and fertilizer in which plants are grown to be transplanted into the Dutch aquarium. In the case of *Saururus*, growth is convenient. The head of the mature plant is removed and allowed to float under intense light. Within two weeks, your plants have sprouted. These young plants are then used for the foreground of our Dutch aquarium. When these grow too large, they are removed and the sequence starts again. The larger *Saururus* are used in other parts of the aquarium where the terracing (slope) demands plants of that height. *Saururus* is a plant which needs plenty of light. If it is light-starved it will become stringy and lackluster and will certainly be unfit for the foreground of the aquarium. Because *Saururus* is so fast growing when it has enough light, the substrate must have some clay or other nutrient in it. Plain sand or gravel has absolutely nothing that a plant can use as a nutrient. Add fertilizer to the substrate if you want phenomenal looking *Saururus*. Your pet shop can supply you with aquarium fertilizer.

You should really learn as much as you can about *Saururus* because it can be used in almost every aquarium situation, even mixed with other plants, because it is so bright green when healthy and the leaves are so nicely formed.

LOBELIA CARDINALIS

Lobelia cardinalis is a frequently used foreground plant. Because it is a stalk plant and a bog plant (just like *Saururus*), it is often used in the aquarium. However, *Lobelia* is not suitable as a foreground plant, it is slightly too large and obscures too much of the front view and combats the sloping affect we are trying to achieve to create the feeling of depth in our Dutch aquarium.

To grow properly, *Lobelia cardinalis* requires a substrate with unwashed gravel which

Lobelia cardinalis is frequently used as a foreground plant because it is a stalk plant and a bog plant.

Perhaps you can allow a few *Lobelia* to grow out of the tank and actually flower.

contains some peat and clay. Being a bog plant it needs a lot of light. Under water it grows much more slowly than when grown under bog conditions (*bog conditions* are when the plant is rooted in soaking wet mud covered by less than an inch (2 cm) of water, with the leaves growing in the air). When *Lobelia* grows properly, the leaves are almost an inch (2 cm) broad and 2 inches (5 cm) long, including the stem.

Lobelia in the aquarium requires constant pruning. If planted in bunches, which should be about 3 inches tall, constant pruning is required. The plants should not be allowed to reach the surface of the water. They should always be an inch below the water's surface. To keep them from growing quickly, remove their roots before planting them in the aquarium. As they develop roots, they will also develop new shoots on the old stalks. These new shoots are removed when they reach about an inch or two (up to 5 cm). However, if possible and practical, leave the plant alone and let nature take its course. Sometimes pruning or picking off the *Lobelia's* new leaves injures the root, which might be catastrophic for the plant.

Using *Lobelia* in the foreground can be effective with constant pruning as you can see from the accompanying photograph. When used as a front plant (foreground plant), the tops of the plants must be constantly pinched back (*beheaded!*). In this way new shoots will appear and they can be left alone until they get too large, at which time you may have to rework the entire area with new, young *Lobelia* produced in your ancillary aquarium. If you really want to produce lots of *Lobelia*, start a large swamp or bog tank. The substrate of the bog must be potting soil (for house plants), mixed with large sized aquarium gravel, which is about 6 mm or 1/4 inch long. The substrate should be muddy or even barely covered with water. With enough light and plant food, the *Lobelia* can easily grow to a height of 250 cm (that's over 8 feet tall!!!). It's flowers are a beautiful red and have an interesting shape. Perhaps you can allow a few to grow out of the tank and actually flower! Once they flower, cut the flower and put it into a small vase. Now cut the large, thick stalk into many pieces of about an inch or two (2-5 cm) and allow them to float. Once an aquarist also added some apple snails to the aquarium. The snails quickly ate the bark of the stalk but for some reason ignored the new leaves that began to grow from the stalk. Each piece of stalk began to generate new leaves and one stalk can produce 250 new plants!

Because of this growth potential, do not plant *Lobelia*, too closely together. Each leaf needs its own source of strong light. If you plant them too closely, some leaves will shade others and the plant will grow poorly from a visual point of view. The *Lobelia* in your aquarium must have all of its leaves bright green. The leaves in the shade will turn light green and then brown and eventually die. You don't want this to happen, so you plant them less densely.

ELATINE MACROPODA

An extraordinarily useful plant, not often seen in pet shops, is *Elatine macropoda*. This plant does well against the front glass with the sloping gravel making it appear taller as it recedes from the front glass, where it can meet up with a dense planting of a taller plant. *Elatine* has the same light and nutrient requirements as *Lobelia* and *Saururus*. This plant has leaves of almost a half inch (1 cm), which grow on thin stalks and creep along the bottom. While it does best in soft water with a pH above 7.2, it has been known to thrive in harder water with as much hardness as 12° German hardness (DH). The stalks of this plant are very delicate and break easily when handled. Use small planting tongs (tweezers).

ECHINODORUS TENELLUS

Another plant that builds interesting foreground mats is the dwarf swordplant known scientifically as *Echinodorus tenellus*. It reproduces quickly and easily by runners. As with the previously mentioned plants, this plant needs lots of light and some fertilization. Because they are so fast growing, plant them initially 2 inches (5 cm) apart. Use large tweezers to plant them so the roots are not torn apart. DO NOT USE *ECHINODORUS TENELLUS* WITH OTHER PLANTS THAT REPRODUCE BY RUNNERS. Otherwise the plants will intrude upon each others growing space. If the adventitious roots infiltrate other areas (where your initial design has it reserved for some other plant), take a long-handled scissors and cut the

Heteranthera zosterifolia is a favorite aquarium plant because it is so readily available, and grows well without a special fertilizer or substrate.

adventitious (wandering) roots and remove them from the tank.

HETERANTHERA ZOSTERIFOLIA

Heteranthera zosterifolia is a favorite aquarium plant because it is so easily available and grows well without a special fertilizer or substrate. It does, however, need a lot of light, as do most fast-growing plants. To keep the plant small, we continuously behead it (pinch it back). New shoots will constantly reappear at the site of the detachment. It is best to behead the plant about one inch (2 cm) from the bottom. In this way a deep, bright green field will develop. *Heteranthera* can easily be used to butt against other short plants, or even against large, taller plants, as shown

in the accompanying photograph. DON'T EXPECT SUCH LUSH GROWTH WITHOUT LOTS OF LIGHT! This is also true for *Prosperinaca pectinata* (=*Hottonia inflata*). Without a lot of light all these plants will do poorly, and instead of presenting a nice foreground lawn for the aquarium, they will present an unimaginably bad impression.

BOLBITIS HEUDELOTII

Bolbitis heudelotii is also easily fastened to walls or bogwood. This African Water Fern can be used in different ways, for example as a shadow provider on the wall, because it also does not need much light. In a strong light it will grow much slower than under moderate light (light-factor

Hemianthus micranthemoides **will give a good shadow to the** *Bolibitis* **that is underneath.**

0.25). We fasten it to a free standing piece of bogwood with which it should have enough space to grow. Under optimal growing conditions this fern becomes rather big, although with some experience it can be held at bay. It is thinned out by cutting the roots. We should be careful when doing this to an older species, because most of the time they are firmly anchored to the bogwood. This plant is very useful as a look-through to intensify depth perception. It not only has contrasting dark green leaves against other plants, but it also grows somewhat "loosely." Therefore, it does not build dark, close groups. If we have a diagonal look-through consisting of bright green plants, in one of the corners, as a "street," then we create a roof at the other end by *B. heudelotii* at three quarters of the height of the wall, or a towering piece of bogwood at the end of the "street." At the top we can have *Hemianthus micranthemoides* grown just underneath the surface of the water, for this needs much light and will shade the *Bolbitis* underneath.

ANUBIAS

We will get the best depth by making the right choice and building an adjoining plant on either side. If we let a bright green "street" go through a group which is a middle green, we use *Anubias nana* and *minima.* We want to use the peculiar way they anchor themselves to a stone by means of their crawling rhizome. In nature they often grow in dense fields at the stony banks of brooks.

The trade offers *Anubias* in small perforated plastic containers, filled with stone- or nylon wool, which comes from a hydroculture. We leave the *Anubias* in the container, take a piece of fern root made as a plank, cut a hole in it the size of the container and fix this together flat on the bottom. Now the container is secured in the hole. The rhizome of the *Anubias* crawls over the fern root and fixes itself. Waste will collect at the same spot, and the *Anubias* will grow excellently when the lighting is right. The plant can be easily moved if necessary.

CRINUM NATANS

In nature, we find *Crinum natans* both at very deep and shallow places. This plant becomes very large and builds a dense tangle of roots, so it can only be used in spacious aquariums. It is best planted in a container with loose sediment with a bit of clay and iron. As a group of plants (three plants are enough!) in a corner of the aquarium, they will grow, dependent on the light, and become strong specimens that will push their leaves along the surface of the water. It is not well suited for an aquarium with a length of one meter and a depth of fifty centimeters.

MIDDLE AND REAR

Let's now go to the middle and rear of the aquarium. The foreground and middle part can easily run into each other, but can also be firmly separated at certain spots. This is the same for the middle and rear parts. This also depends, among other things, on whether we have the bottom sloping gradually to the rear and we do not use terraces. Of course, there is the difference in taste. Therefore, I will point out a few possibilities in which I will think first of solitary plants, not of group plants. Therefore, we have at our disposal the following species: *Anubias*, *Aponogeton*, *Cryptocoryne*, *Echinodorus*, and *Hygrophila*, just to name the most important ones.

We know *Hygrophila* as a group plant, with the exception of *Hygrophila stricta*. Underneath good lighting, a single stalk stays nice and stocky. With its long, pointed and bright green leaves, it is an excellent plant to contrast before a dark background. *Hygrophila stricta* works wonders in a flat field, as does *Echinodorous tenellus*, with a background of *Bolbitis heudelotii*, bogwood, etc. They can also be planted as a middle part of the aquarium, and then leave open swimming room behind it. They often grow side shoots. If they become too bushy, just cut the shoots and plant them again. This plant is effective as a group in the rear. Depending on the size of the aquarium, we use slim and tall growing, or solitary plants that grow more in width. In roomy tanks, *Anubias congensis* looks good in an open space, if we remove the old leaves standing away from the stalk. It still grows well in medium hard water (12°dH) and under average light (factor 0.4), however it needs a nutrient rich, thick bottom layer, thus it looks best a little further into the middle part. Young, tall growing specimens we surround, for example, with *Saururus cernuus*, and also, because of the contrast of form and color, with *Cryptocoryne becketii*, which will grow as high as 15 centimeters under the same good light. In this way we hide the stalk of *A. congensis*, and look at a nice tall growing group.

CRYPTOCORYNE

We use the same principle with *Cryptocoryne ciliata* as a free standing solitary plant. Once planted, *C. ciliata* should be left in peace. Often the plant will flower when left alone in the same place for three years or more. Self pollination of the flower under water will produce a fruit with over 40 seeds. These are scattered on a very loose bottom made out of gravel with a diameter of 4 millimeters and mixed with some clay. We leave the height of the water at approximately 4 centimeters, and light it well for at least 12 hours a day. As soon as the leaves reach the surface of the water, we heighten the water level somewhat. Older plants of *C. ciliata*, which stand always at the same spot in the aquarium, also reproduce vegetatively. In this way they become, over the years, a very nice group. Out of the axil of most of the dying leaves, young plants will grow. However, if the leaves turn

Culture outside the water can work very well to grow *Cryprocoryne zewaldae*.

Cyrptocoryne zewaldae **in nature also does not like harsh light.**

yellow do not remove them at once, but wait. When the old leaf is completely rotted away, we do not tear off the young plants right away, for they are about 5 centimeters and have no roots. We plant the young plants very carefully in a raising tank. Unwashed sand will be enough. We thank the Dutch hobbyist *Vlasblom* for the first instructions on how to propagate *C. ciliata*. He even grew a triplet shoot. He then planted the shoot with several structures in the bottom. At the top the young plant developed with roots. If there were enough roots, he cut off the shoot just below where the roots grew, planted it and left the rest of the shoot. Often one or two more offshoots then developed out of the nodes.

As a rule we should leave *Cryptocoryne* in peace, because after replanting they take some time to build new roots and runners. With *C. becketti, C. parva, C. undulata, C. walkeri, C. wendtii* and *C. zewaldae* the culture outside the water works very well. We plant them in containers with a mix of unwashed sand, some soil for flowers, and peat, then put the container in water just as far as the top of the soil and pay attention to the heat and humidity. Almost all of the named species endure the sun very well. *C. willisii* (the old *nevillii*) loves a little diffuse light, just like *C. zewaldae*, which in nature also does not like harsh light. In a culture outside the water, the plants build either faster (*C. becketii*) or slower (*C. zewaldae*) large amounts of roots, or far reaching runners. Many species of *Cryptocoryne* have various forms, and we know three forms, that differ in length and width of their leaves. We also know of three forms with *C. becketii*, and especially *C. wendtii* that have very variable forms in leaves and color. In our aquarium the low growing *C. wendtii* is the nicest. From the genus *Cryptocoryne* we have another beautiful solitary plant named *C. crispatula*. It is best suited for somewhat deeper (50 to 60 centimeters) aquariums. We buy the plants small, as they are mostly offered at a length of approximately 15 to 30 centimeters. We plant them in a free space in the middle part, and under good light they will reach a height of approximately 50 centimeters and put out runners. If these are somewhat grown we cut them off, plant them again close to the mother plant, and

Cryptocoryne wendtii **has very variable forms in leaves and color. The low growing** *Cryptocoryne wendtii* **is the nicest.**

in this way create a beautiful solitary group. With this plant we can interrupt a large swimming space, so that the fish have to swim around it. As an eye catching object this plant, two centimeters in width, band shaped, and with middle green colored leaves, is highly decorative.

APONOGETON

The same is possible with *Aponogeton undulatus,* although it does not grow runners. Because of the small form of the leaves *A. undulatus* works very decoratively. Its method of multiplying is interesting. It develops small bulbs on a stalk, which is where the young plants grow out of. We should not remove them right away, but should wait until more of them have grown with enough roots. Often only one young plant grows out of each stalk.

Unlike *A. undulatus, A. ulvaceus* is a giant, with corrugated leaves that are 5 centimeters broad and about 30 centimeters long. As a solitary plant it needs much more room. This goes also for the smaller *A. echinatus.* We cover the stalks of these species by a half circle of low growing plants, although the bottom of the stalk should have a space of approximately 10 centimeters in diameter. *A. ulvaceus* fits perfectly in low growing groups, as its leaves curve as a broad crown over the other plants. *A. echinatus* and *ulvaceus* are often confused by many aquarists. If they flower, then this mistake is impossible. *A. echinatus* has a single axil and a white spadix, whereas *A. ulvaceus* has a double axil which, because of its more than rich pollen, looks yellow.

Species of *Aponogeton* need a rest period just as *Barclaya* and *Nymphea* species. With many species it is necessary to move the bulbs across the bottom or they will die, for instance, like *A. boivinianus.* This very beautiful plant, which is only useful in large aquariums, should never be planted too closely to other plants. *Aponogeton* should never be planted too close to the wall, because they do not develop too well. This works better with *Ottelia alismoides,* which in the aquarium is used as a solitary plant, but also can be used at the sides. This difficult plant needs warmth and good light. Very clear water is a necessity, and the soil should be nourishing. To get this we mix unwashed sand, clay peat, and pot soil in even parts. If well lit, the plant will flower in the aquarium.

ECHINODORUS

The genus *Echinodorus* offers the most species for solitary or group planting. They have many different leaf forms. The narrow leafed Amazon Sword Plant, *E. amazonicus,* which, in larger aquariums, are also used as a group plant, is well known. Others are *E. bleheri,* the broad leafed Amazon Sword

Because of the small form of the leaves *Aponogeton undulatus* works very decoratively.

Echinodorus cordifolius has nice oval leaves which look like rosettes and is the most decorative in a free space, or resting against a corner on a terrace wall.

Plant, a typical solitary plant in the open space, or alone upon a terrace in the middle of a bloom of *E. maior* (formarly *E. martii*) or *E. osiris.* The red Amazon Sword Plant and *E. berteroi*, the beautiful cellophane-plant, which also needs much room, especially when standing alone, works very decoratively. It is not good to have a plant jammed into a group.

Totally different leaf forms are found in *E. cordifolius* (formerly *E. radicans*) and *E. radicalis. Echinodorus* is a swamp plant that grows taller than one meter. Nevertheless,

it is useful in the aquarium, as we nurse it as a wreathed form. For best results we grow it in a soil of unwashed, or even washed sand. It is best planted in a container, otherwise if left to grow freely it will send its roots everywhere. If we then want to remove it from the aquarium, it will become chaotic. As soon as the plants grow leaves on their long stems, we should cut them immediately. *E. cordifolius* has nice oval leaves that look like rosettes. It is the most decorative in an open space or resting against a corner on a terrace wall.

E. horizontalis has fewer problems. The leaves are in the form of a heart and grow almost at a 90 degree angle from the stem. For this reason, we are able to recognize the plant immediately. It needs more light than *E. cordifolius*, and should stand free and be left in peace. Just like all Amazon Sword Plants, *E. horizontalis* grows a flower on which young shoots develop. When these are strong and have grown some roots, we can cut them. *E. cordifolius, E. maior,* and *E. osiris* are propagated in the same way. To avoid further growth difficulties, we bend the stem with the young plants to the bottom and anchor them with stones. If they grow further, we should push them a little deeper, so that the plants have their roots right on the bottom. We leave them alone for approximately three months, at which time they become strong enough and we can plant them in another spot, where the light intensity is right. No species of *Echinodorus* should be planted too deeply. If there are not enough old roots to plant, we carefully tie them to a stone or a piece of lead, which is carefully folded around the foot of the stalk. Then we protect it with a piece of polystyrene.

GROUP PLANTS

Now here are some examples of decorative plants that are especially suitable as groups. First of all, species of *Alternanthera* are suitable, because of their reddish to purple-reddish color, as a contrast group. It can be said, however, for all reddish plants, that we use them only sparingly, because they work negatively against the rest of the plants. For example, *Nymphea lotus*, which is known with totally red leaves, is used solely for decorative and striking effect. All red plants need a lot of light. Another well known one is *Ammania senegalensis*, which grows best in softer water and should not be planted in a newly decorated aquarium. In good light it shows its beautiful gold/brown color. It grows well, as so many plants do, under a combination of Phillips TLD 83 and Gro-Lux

***Nymphea lotus* is known with totally red leaves and then is used solely for decorative and striking effect.**

or Osram Fluora L. Next, we remove the three lower pairs of leaves and put it carefully in the planting hole, one stem per hole about seven centimeters apart. Its soil should consist of unwashed sand and 20% clay loam. It reacts well to iron based fertilizer. We take a piece of approximately ten centimeters from the top and plant this. The old stalk is left floating at the surface of the water, and from the shoulders of the leaves new young plants will appear, which can grow in an emersed way.

Ammania gracilis should be planted further apart, because under good light the leaves will reach a length of a good ten centimeters, and they should not be shaded. With

enough light the leaves appear a nice red, with less light they become green. The bottom soil should contain clay and iron fertilizer, which is also essential. The plant is easily propagated in a swamp culture, but here it will exhibit quite a different shaped leaf. After taking off the top, two new shoots will appear at the cut. In addition, the plant will grow side shoots, which can be cut off when needed. If we do not pay attention to the light, soil mixture, and the hardness of the water, we will loose a valuable plant for the aquarium.

BACOPA

Species of *Bacopa* offer smaller or larger groups in the margin, or even standing free.

***Bacopa caroliniana* looks bright green, middle green with reddish veins, or completely red depending on the care taken.**

Bacopa caroliniana (syn. *B. lamplexicaulis*) is better as *B. monnieri*, which likes it a bit cooler, although it is also found in Southeast Asia. *B. Caroliniana* looks bright green, middle green with reddish veins or completely red, depending on the care taken. Both species need lots of light, and we should plant their stems one by one.

CAMBOMBA

With *Cambomba*- species we plant three stalks in each plant hole. *Cabomba caroliniana* is the easiest, *C. aquatica* is more difficult, and *C. furcata* (syn. *C. piahyensis*,) the red *Cabomba*, often gives problems. They all demand crystal clear water, free of particles. In addition, the latter three need soft water. Red *Cambomba* often dies after the planting, but the rest can have roots again and give new shoots, which will flower under Phillips TLD 83. They should not be overshadowed by other species.

CRYPTOCORYNE

If we plant groups of *Cryptocoryne* for decorating an aquarium, it is better to wait until the aquarium is settled. When decorating an aquarium for the first time it is best to use fast growing cheap plants, for instance *Hygrophila polysperma, Certapteris cornuta* (syn. *C. thalictroides*), *Hygrophila difformis* (syn. *Synnema triflorum*), and such.

Then we let the aquarium be without fish, start later with only a few species, and slowly build the number of fish. After approximately three months, when it is clear that the plants will grow well, we start to plant *Cryptocoryne*. Good advice is not to have the light at full strength, but if possible, use a low light and then increase the wattage slowly. If we have another aquarium, which is well settled and with some free space, we put the purchased *Cryprocoryne* in this aquarium for the time being. You should never remove the plants after a short time, if we interrupt the building of roots in such a short period, it often works negatively.

Red Cabomba can have roots and give new shoots, which will flower under TLD 83.

***Cryptocoryne petchii* contrasts very well with *Prosperpinaca pectinata*.**

Most *Cryptocoryne* are planted in groups. Many species grow fast and without any problems, for instance *C. affinis* becomes taller under less light, but very stocky under more light. *C. becketii, C. wendtii, C. petchii, C. willisii, C. walkeri, C. cordata, C. crispatula, C. usteriana, C. pupurea,* and *C. griffithii* all are decorative plants for larger groups. Usually they need less light, however they are very sensitive to the notorious *Cryptocoryne* rotting.

As *Cryptocoryne* reacts very negatively to great disturbances, we should avoid sudden changes in light intensity, and change old lamps for new ones very gradually. Regular water changes will make them less sensitive. If you rarely change the water, and then change a

great amount suddenly, then many species will rot. Dense stocks, for instance of *C. willisii* or *C. beckettii,* are not thinned out after one year. Then you will be flabbergasted how many young plants you will have. If you cut all the roots supplied with knots and let them float on pieces of 2 centimeters, young plants will often appear, which we should allow to grow roots before we plant them.

ELEOCHARIS ACICULARIS

Eleocharis acicularis is very usable as a wall made out of plants as shown on the left hand side in the picture. It needs clear water, not too much light (danger of algae!), and will grow in different heights, often just as a five centimeter high "lawn," but often as high as 15

centimeters. It is planted (with a pair of tweezers) in small bushes with approximately two centimeters in between. By means of outlets, it will build a dense stock. We should make sure that it will not mix with neighboring plants. These runners are removed, and if it still becomes too dense we must remove some of the plants.

HYGROPHILA

Species of *Hygrophila*, like *Cabomba*, can be reproduced. We put *H. polysperma*, but also many other plants with supple stalks, onto the bottom and weigh down the ends to prevent the plant from upending itself. Young plants will emerge from each leaf axil. When they become approximately ten centimeters long, we cut the stalk. However, do not pinch off the young plants! In this way, we will have a large stock from just a few stalks.

H. corymbosa (syn. *Nomaphila stricta*) is easily reproduced if we remove the top and leave the old stalk. Shoots will develop from here, even at the breaking spot of the stalk. At approximately 8 centimeters we take the rooted shoots off and plant them. *H. corymbosa* needs room to develop and should not be planted too closely together. In the larger aquariums, we plant them in rows and shift the planting holes.

LIMNOPHILA AQUATICA

Limnophila aquatica is the best known *Limnophila* species. In each plant hole we put one stalk, about 6 centimeters apart and shift the rows. This plant needs a great deal of light and not too hard, clear water, then it will leave garlands that are over ten centimeters broad. We give this very beautiful group plant unwashed sand with an additional 30% clay. It often suffers from chlorosis. In that case iron based fertilizer is necessary.

LUDWIGIA

Also, with the *Ludwigia* species we plant only one stalk in a plant hole 4 centimeters apart, and shift the rows. When the light is hot enough it often loses its lower leaves. Good strong light produces green to red/brown leaves with strong reddish undersides. They are easy to multiply, as it forms many side shoots. If the bush becomes too thick, we should thin it out. An addition of iron fertilizer works wonders.

MYRIOPHYLLUM

Myriophyllum species in general have great light demands. *Myriophyllum matogrossense* demands the most light. It reacts very strongly to floating particles in the water, becomes soiled quickly and then dies. This species is best used on a higher terrace. If we leave it to grow as garlands out of the corner or somewhere out of the fringe plants, it does not work very decoratively, but does serve as a spawning place for those inhabitants that live at the surface of the water, such as *Epiplatys* species. *M. aquaticum* (syn. *M. brasiliense*) is less sensitive, has green leafed garlands, and can, as all species from this order, be planted with three stalks in

one plant hole. If they grow at the surface of the water, the *Myriophyllum* species often grow side shoots, so that we have to thin them or they develop too strongly.

NAJAS

Species of *Najas* should not be planted. We keep them at the bottom with a small piece of lead foil that is carefully wrapped around a

Limnophila aquatica is the best-known Limnophila species.

few stalks with a piece of foam material. Very carefully we let them sink onto a terrace, as most of the *Najas* are very fragile and are, as a rule, only used as floating plants. However, they build beautiful free standing groups in the fringe areas with the lead method. The nicest species is *Najas microdon*, which not only looks decorative, but also offers spawning areas for many fish species and refuge for young fish, just like other floating plants.

ROTALA

A completely different form of leaves than already discussed, is seen in *Rotala wallichii* and is shown by *Rotala macrantha*. It is too bad that this very decorative plant is not very easy to grow, but perseverance and effort will be rewarded by beautiful red/brown to pink colored leaves. We should plant the stalks five centimeters apart, one by one, and shift the rows. They need good light. If given it, they grow very well, and even build garlands along the surface of the water. They do not like shade (see the picture), and also the leaves of stalks that stand beside each other should not hinder each other. *Rotala* needs a soil with an addition of clay and iron based fertilizer. It breaks easily and should be planted with care.

VALLISNERIA

Besides the already mentioned species, I would like to name *Vallisneria gigantea*, the green giant, and *V. neotropicalis*, the red giant. They both can only be used in large aquariums in a corner. Under enough light, their leaves grow along the surface of the water, but they take light away from the plants that grow underneath. They demand water that is medium hard. In general, all aquarium plants can be damaged when planting, and they often die. A plant should never just be pushed into the bottom, but a hole should be made with a finger, the plant carefully put in, and the hole

Takashi Amano is the father of the Nature Aquarium concept, whose groundbreaking work, *Nature Aquarium World,* was published by T.F.H. in 1994. He takes his inspiration from natural scenes such as this mossy stream. This particular scene was used by Amano to design "convex" aquascapes in which the center is fuller than the edges, in much the same way as the plant-covered log here arches through the field of view. Photo by Takashi Amano.

closed gently. We cut the roots of all plants with a sharp knife. Depending on the species, we remove one to three pairs of leaves and plant the stalk as far as 5 centimeters into the bottom. All species are planted in such a way that the root is just covered. The roots are not removed, because they anchor the plant into the bottom. If this does not work, we can use a piece of lead foil.

***Rotala wallichii* is a very decorative plant that is not too easy to grow and maintain.**

ALGAE

Especially in the beginning, it is important to choose fast growing plants. Depending on the growth of the plants and on their density, much less algae will grow. Important factors to prevent the growing of algae are: Partly changing the water, not too many fishes, appropriate feeding and the removal of the food remains. Nevertheless, there is no recipe against the growth of algae. Indeed, algae eaters sometimes will help, but against the feared blue-green algae it helps to grow *Ceratophyllum demersum* along the surface of the water.

Chemical means are the last resort. Patience, stamina, and experience will especially pay off here!

Not all algae are harmful. Green thread algae indicates a very healthy aquarium. However, they can grow wild over stocks of *Cryptocoryne willisii* and be a nuisance for *Cabomba* and such. For this reason, we remove them from the beginning as much as possible. We just roll the algae on a rough little stick, and pull them out of the aquarium.

We do not like to see algae in the aquarium. Of course, there are exceptions, like the nice green paintbrush algae, which often settle on wood, cork bark, and also on the shells of apple snails. This works very decoratively! They also develop on healthy and older leaves of certain plants, like the *Echinodorus* species or also on *Anubias*. The leaves overgrown with those algae are best removed.

We can say that in most cases the fight against algae is very difficult. The fight must be done in such a way that the cause of the algae is also removed. In aquaristic circles, algae are often the cause of heated discussions. It is obviously much better to be ahead of the growth of algae instead of fighting them when they are already settled. In many cases, we can prevent it if we start the aquarium in the right way: Using fast growing plants, a moderate number of fish, exact measuring of food, changing of the water, avoiding any burden in the water, the right material for building walls, and terraces could all be deciding factors if algae will appear or not.

Experience shows that perseverance pays off, for after one year with regular changes of water once a week algae will recede. Do not reach for chemical preparations to fight the algae! However, I do not wish to say that there are no good preparations. Useful directions, in which it is told in exactly what water conditions this preparation can be used, or in what conditions they cannot be used, and which plants are sensitive to this preparation should be carefully followed. As long as it is not a case in which one aquarist swears that one preparation has "helped very well and that the real plants did not suffer," and another aquarist had a disastrous result with the same preparation.

The manufacturers should oblige all aquarists to everlasting thanks if they would enclose exact specifications with their product, because it is too bad if a wonder in the living room is totally ruined by the wrong specifications.

When using a chemical preparation make sure that the directions are followed exactly as they are stated. Photo courtesy of Aquarium Pharmaceuticals.

THE FISHES

Although, at first we think the slogan "wonder in the living room" refers to an aquarium with esthetically beautiful plant decorations with changing colors, it also refers to the fishes that belong in the aquarium. In decorating an

for a certain balance between the number of fishes and healthy plants. In addition, we have the size of the aquarium, the illumination, the water temperature, the healthiness of the water, the feeding process, and the number of bacteria all

function correctly. The combination of fish and plants is very important. Real water plants play a completely different role than the swamp plants, which are mostly used by us. Real water plants produce more oxygen when the environment is right, and most of the time they grow faster. If we have a lot of those plants in our aquarium, then the starting position is quite different than in an aquarium with swamp plants. This again influences the fish community which has been chosen.

> ## "We should look for a certain balance between the number of fish and healthy plants..."

aquarium we can take two paths. First, we can choose to occupy ourselves with decorations composed of plants and think about which fishes we would like to have afterwards. Most of the time we choose a group of fish that we think are beautiful due to their form, shape and/or color. Then it is unimportant if the animals in this aquarium do nothing else than swim back and forth. The other option is to first think about the fishes we would like to care for. Then their beauty does not come first, but more their natural behavior in building a territory or the way they display during courtship and spawning. Of course, this fish community can also be very appealing. In this case the choice of plants is made afterwards, but with the functional use of certain species of plants, and how to group them together, in mind.

It is important that we know how many fishes can be accomodated. We should look

playing an important role in the total life process. Every factor is as important as the other. If one is not correct, it can be the reason why our aquarium community will not

In the esthetically pleasing aquarium we combine plants and fishes. In reality, many aquarists follow the ratio of one

Frozen foods offer a wide range of choices to the aquarist. Photo courtesy of Ocean Nutrition.

gram of fish to two liters of water for small species, and one gram of fish to three or four or more liters of water when it is a larger fish. With the larger growing species an important issue is—how much food they digest and how much detritus has to be broken down. The rule of so many grams of fish per so much water is actually very inadequate, and can be confusing for beginners.

We should ask ourselves how much room a fish needs on the basis of its behavior, and we will find that out quickly enough: The more water the animal has at its disposal the better it is. Surely, there is a bottom line, otherwise we could hardly hold any fish in our aquarium. Often enough the hobbyist draws the line.

One may find a small number of fishes boring, while another may be completely content with them. You could have a very beautiful aquarium with a length of one and a half meters in which there are only four to six Discus, or a nice school of *Puntius tetrazona*, or a collection of a number of species. Here tastes are

You could have a very beautiful aquarium with a length of one and a half meters, in which there are only four to six Discus.

different. There is rarely a hobbyist who will enjoy looking behind the tail of a fish to see another. In this case we arrive at the other point.

In many cases the question of whether it is a 'schooling fish' or not plays a role. Of course, this also depends on the size of the aquarium. When a fish is not a 'schooling fish', it does not mean that two of them are enough. It is true that such species more or less live their own lives, but they also like to choose their partner when they spawn. Therefore, even from those species we buy more of the notorious 'spawning pairs.'

If you only put a community together from species that you like, the functional combination of fishes and plants does not play a role. The number of fishes and the form of the society almost always means that in this aquarium nothing interesting happens. Only when the aquarium is very large will the possibility arise that some fishes will build a territory at a certain spot and will spawn there. This is a stroke of luck that seldom happens.

Therefore, it is better to care for less species with more fish per species, but always less than the normal community aquarium. Aquariums populated by this rule distinguish themselves, and one often finds fry that are born in them. There are no fry without spawning and no spawning without courtship, and there is no courtship when the aquarium environment is not suitable. Actually, there is no suitable aquarium environment if we do not know what the fishes prefer. Without this knowledge it often

Puntius tetrazona **is a nice schooling fish that looks very beautiful in an aquarium. Photo by K. Knaack.**

happens that aquariums are supplied with wrong decorations. In this case, we may choose the wrong plants, put the right plants in the wrong spot, or choose the wrong lighting. The delight we could have from the aquarium never occurs. The sad thing about this is that we often do not know that we could have something completely different, namely an aquarium that can be fascinating and have the correct environment.

ILLUMINATION

Now we suddenly have arrived at another road, because what is "wrong lighting"? The fundamental lighting of a Dutch tank is related to the plants, but now we are referring to the fishes. Here we can ask ourselves if an aquarium could be illuminated too strongly. There are several starting points to answer this question.

Many aquarists point to the

fierce lighting in the tropics, which is much stronger than we have to offer our plants. This may be true but these aquarists are thinking about the plants, and the fishes only play a minor part.

Other aquarists consider the fishes more, but also include the plants. They already have the knowledge that many plant species will thrive with much less light. Typical examples are: Java fern *(Microsorium pteropus)* and *Anubias barteri* var. *nana*, which will clearly have trouble at a light quantity that we need for a lush growth of Java moss *(Vesicularia dubyana)*. Do we turn down the illumination? If so, the Java moss *(Vesicularia dubyana)* will grow less lush, but the Java fern will grow well.

When we look into an aquarium in which the illumination is very strong (for the plants that need strong light), then we can observe that many fishes do not look as

colorful as they should. Even when the aquarium is healthy, functions well, and is well cared for, Bleeding Heart Tetras *(Hyphessobrycon erythrostigma)* do not show as much red as they should. The beautiful pastel tints are absent from *Hemigrammus ocellifer*, and even more so with *Hemigrammus pulcher* or *Hemigrammus caudovittatus*. This is also the case with *Hemmigrammus rhodostomus* and *Petitella georgiae*. A school of those fishes should not be combined with *Paracheirodon axelrodi*. When both schools mix together none of them show to their best advantage. There is more than one kind of

Above: The beautiful pastel tints are absent from *Hemigrammus ocellifer.* Photo by A. Roth. *Below:* Even when the aquarium is healthy, functions well, and is well cared for the Bleeding Hearts do not appear as red as they could. Photo by M. P. & C. Piednoir.

A school of either *Hemigrammus rhodostomus* or *Petitella georgiae* should not be mixed with *Paracheirodon axelrodi*, because their best colors will not show. Photos by H.-J. Richter.

fish species that normally swim at lower, middle, or upper water layers. Moreover, many fishes behave shyly, something they normally do not do.

We call fishes "shy" when they withdraw among the plants. A typical example is the pretty *Puntius fasciolans* of Africa, or *Poecilocharax weitzmani* of South America. Very often we see how these species are withdrawing to an open spot between the plants, where the lighting is not as harsh as it is at other spots in the aquarium. Of course the "shyness" can also have other causes than poor lighting. A too small aquarium, or a wrongly combined fish community could also be the cause. If we leave this out of consideration, then the lighting is more often thought guilty than it naturally is.

I still speak of a normal and not of a so called "functional" community aquarium. A wonder in the living room with a beautiful, healthy plant balance is only truly beautiful when we also are concerned with the fishes. They should be living as a colorful contrasting point against the stillness of the rest. However, liveliness and color are influenced by light.

How does this appear in nature? We will give a few examples, otherwise we would need a completely new article about light.

Many fish live in very clear waters, which are exposed to the sun almost the whole day, and these waters can look everything from colorless to cola colored, or darker. At the banks we often find a very thick vegetative growth. Grasses and other plants hang into the water, but at the border we often find water plants or swamp plants. In other parts, these waters are, at least for a part of the day, in

When an embankment is densely grown with swamp plants, then there is only diffuse light at a depth of 20 to 30 centimeters.

Above: A typical example of a "shy" fish is *Poecilocharax weitzmani*, which wll withdraw into a secluded space in the aquarium. Photo by H.-J. Richter. *Below: Paracheirodon axelrodi* is one of the most popular fish to use in a Dutch aquarium because it does not bother other fishes or eat any of the plant life.

shadows or even in deep shadows, so that there are only a few water plants or none at all. All these habitats are separated into surface zone, bottom zone, embankment zone, and open water zone. Many fishes are found in all zones, and often the adults and juveniles are separate. There are also species that only live in a certain zone, and other species that are not to be found there.

The light in these zones is mostly of varying intensity. At the surface of the open water we find the highest intensity and at the bottom much less. When the embankment has a dense growth of swamp plants, then there is only

Above: Danio aequipinnatus **was found in clear water. Photo by M.P. & C. Piednoir.** *Below:* **The waterfall is from Sri Lanka during the dry season; it contradicts the jungle biotope.**

Above: In the stagnant slow moving water these *Belontia signata* were found together with the *Danio aequipinnatus. Below:* In Southeast Asia *Rasbora borapetensis* live in very different habitats. Photos by M. P. & C. Piednoir.

diffuse light at a depth of 20 to 30 centimeters. Cola colored water filters out even more light. Strong light above the water does not mean that it is as light everywhere in the water. There we find the border zone. This is where the light is less in much overshadowed jungle brooks with very cola colored water, where we often find very specific plants, or no plants at all in the water.

The waterfall was photographed in the dry season in Sri Lanka, and contradicts a jungle biotope. In the clear water we found *Danio aequipinnatus* and in the stagnant or slow moving sections we found it together with adult *Belontia signata*! In Southeast Asia we will find *Rasbora*, *Puntius* and *Danio* species, which if we talk about them in relationship to the light, live in very different habitats. Many only live in certain habitats, which are often in the shade, or flow through cola colored water, or live in water that is mixed with loam particles, so that we cannot see our hand anymore at a depth of 20 centimeters. Here they live in the upper water parts, but also at a depth of more than 1 meter. I will name only one *Rasbora heteromorpha*, that can be found in the darkest cola colored water. Here they look unbelievably red, just like *Rasbora kalochroma*, which can be so red that they look

Rasbora heteromorpha can be found in the darkest cola colored water, and here they look unbelievably red. Photo by M. P. & C. Piednoir.

Puntius species can hardly be found in cola colored water, and they are mostly encountered at a depth of at least 50 centimeters under the water surface, or in the upper part where there are enough plants. Photo by Dr. Herbert R. Axelrod

almost black. In nature, *Rasbora heteromorpha* can also be found in much clearer, colorless water, but there they are less colorful. *Puntius tetrazona* is an example of a fish that can be found in many different habitats, but they usually show the same color. *Puntius pentazona*, or *P. hexazona* can hardly be found in cola colored water, and mostly at a depth of at least 50 centimeters under the water surface, or in the upper part where there are enough plants. For instance, in the aquarium we accompany *Danio aequipipinnatus*, for the upper and middle parts of a larger aquarium, with *Puntius pentazona*, which will not be as colorful when nothing is done about the lighting and the color of the bottom.

In principle, it can be said that all fishes with a deep, dark red, brownish red, or blackish red body color come from a dark environment. There are also other grounds on which these fishes never show their optimal color, if we do not apply special methods, like filtering through peat, or dimmed lighting, and such. This is very difficult to accomplish in an aquarium in the living room. So, we have to look for a compromise, or put together a very special fish community.

To compromise means that we must choose plants that need less light, and in this way accommodate the fishes. However, this reduces the choice of plants. It is too bad that these fast growing plants need a lot of light. In smaller aquariums nothing works except to combine such plants with fishes that tolerate less light. A mixture is rarely possible.

In larger aquariums, of 100 centimeters or more, it is possible to create shade and diffuse light as well as very well lit places. This can, for instance, be accomplished through plants that grow along the water surface, like *Myriophyllum, Rotala,* and many kinds of *Vallisneria.* Floating plants are less suitable, because they multiply too rapidly and we have to restrict them to a certain spot at the surface. The simplest thing to do is to use *Ceratopteris cornuta and Ceratopteris pteroides.* Their bushy roots can be pinned to the Styropor wall or to a floating piece of cork, which can be held in place by a thin bamboo shoot that gets fastened between the front and rear panes. This is done in such a way that the cork is pushed underwater a bit and held in place. Also, a piece of bogwood can be used. A piece of bogwood overgrown with Java fern (*Microsorium pteropus*), *Vesicularia dubyana* (Java-moss) or *Bolbitis heudelotii,* or with pinned down floating plants will create shadows or diffused light spots in the aquarium, especially at the top side of the open swimming space. This idea provides many possibilities, which moreover can be supported by a dark colored bottom or one that is overgrown. In the diffused light areas we plant those plants that stay low, and that do not need too much light.

We can get a very nice dark bottom when we spread basalt chips on the bottom layer of coarse sand. We can also mix both ingredients and just put them on the bottom and combine them with low growing plants like *Cryptocoryne parva, Echinodorus tenellus,* etc. This works on almost all fishes in a calming way, and they will also show better colors.

I would advise against using a peat filter, for this filter will color the water brown and much more light is needed to penetrate the water.

Therefore, we come to an

Aquarium:	200x50x50 cm
Light hood:	5 cm high
Lighting:	1 Philips TL 65W/32
past:	1 Philips TL 65W/33
	2 Philips TL 8W/33
later:	1 Philips 'TL'D 58W/83 (12 hours)
	1 Philips 'TL'D 58W/84 (9 hours)
	2 Philips TL 8W/33 (12 hours)
Decoration:	bogwood between the plants, highest terrace 15 cm. Walls of Styropor, painted in several natural colors, partially grown over with Vesicularia dubyana.
Filter:	1 week per month. Every week 20% fresh water.

Plants used in the setup above:

Hygrophila stricta
Hygrophila difformis
Rotala rotundifolia
Lobelia cardinalis
Aponogeton undulatus
Cryptocoryne becketii
Nymphaea lotus (green, red spotted)
Nymphaea lotus (red)
Heteranthera zosterifolia
Vesicularia dubyana (on walls)
Hydrocoytle leucopetala
Cryptocoryne "petchii"
Aponogeton crispus
Saururus cernuus
Cryptocoryne willisii
Eichhornia azurea
Echinodorus tenellus
Microsorium pteropus
Limnophila aquatica
Ludwigia repens x palustris (with bogwood)
Echinodorus bleheri
Cryptocoryne undulata

aquarium with changes in the lighting that will be appreciated by many fishes. We can rearrange this with ordinary lamps in different wattages. Today this is much more difficult to arrange due to fluorescent lights, for their big disadvantage is that they give a flat uniform light. This light does not liven up the aquarium, so we must help with the grouping of plants. We also can lower the light intensity at certain spots with pieces of cardboard on the cover pane under the fluorescent lights.

Many hobbyists already practice lighting differences as they choose their lamps. In Dutch aquariums we can see that instead of one 36 watt lamp and one 18 watt lamp, three 18 watt lamps are used, because the light quantity is different. Already, many top aquariums have as many lamps in their lighting hoods as necessary. In this way, we have light reserve and we can "play" with light, not only to please the plants, but also to please the fishes.

A normal or common community aquarium is divided into sunny and shady areas, more or less divided swimming room that can especially be accomplished in larger aquariums. In this way, we can establish particular spots that are preferred by many fishes. Thus, we have the transition to the functional aquarium.

The functional aquarium is a new expression. It is defined as: "A functional aquarium is an esthetically and decorative aquarium with plants, in which the plants are grouped in such a way that they invite the fishes to show more of their behavior climaxing in their breeding."

So, before we begin to make a choice of plants, make a drawing of how to plant the aquarium and we should have an idea about the fishes that we want to care for. The starting point is to bring the fishes to breed in the living room aquarium, without having the intention to do so. In this way, it becomes a beautiful aquarium in which we can

Above: Nematobrycon palmeri, a species of tetra, has been known to spontaneously spawn when living in an aquarium. Below: The *Pyrrhulina spilota* male should have a quiet spot in the aquarium where he can build a preserve. Photo by W. Sommer.

Moenkhausia pittieri is a species that prefers dark spots; if these spots are not available it will do nothing in the aquarium. Photo above by M. P. & C. Piednoir, and below by R. Zukal.

observe the lives of our fishes. This means also a limitation in choosing the fishes. If we care for many animals of one kind, then it must always be a community in which the different species disturb each other as little as possible. This is closely related to the size of the aquarium, because in a small aquarium we can only care for one species that lives at the bottom, with a few species gladly laying their eggs in the plants at the edges of the aquarium.

SPAWNING

We should know something about reproductive behavior and the way the fishes will exhibit it. In this way, species from the wild are distinguished from those species that are bred. Species from the wild will need a special tank, or we will have to use a breeding tank.

Let us limit ourselves, in the first place, to the community aquarium mainly with fishes from South America. We can compile a list of many different associations in which oftentimes a fish will one day spawn spontaneously. The tetras, for instance: *Nematobrycon* species and *Inpaichthys kerri, Moenkhausia pittieri, Copella arnoldi,* and many *Pyrrhulina* species. *Nematobrycon, Inpaichthys,* and *Moenkhausia pittieri* are typical examples of species that prefer dark spots. If those spots are not available, they will do nothing. They like to spawn at walls that are overgrown with Java moss or Java fern, but also at spots where the lighting is diffuse, for instance under bushy *Myriophyllum* and even *Blyxa echinosperma.* The sparkling *Moenkhausia pittieri* like to mate in plants at the border region, preferably in plants with fine leaves, but also in *Bacopa, Lobelia,* and *Rotala* leaves. They are not choosy, but prefer diffusely lit spots, and will even spawn in densely grown bottom plants or in

Cryptocoryne species. *Hyphessobrycon callistus* prefer the same conditions as *Moenkhausia pittieri.* *Hasemania nana,* on the other hand, prefer to spawn in the evening, when the lights of the aquarium are turned a little lower. Here, the lowering of the

light intensity plays a role. *Poptella orbicularis* loves to have a sunny, or well lit, aquarium, and will spawn at very well lit spots, many times free in the water, many times close to plants just like *Gymnocorymbus ternetzi.*

So far so good. All this will

Below: *Copella arnoldi* likes to spawn on surfaces that are overgrown wih Java moss or Java fern.

Above:* A cover glass is especially necessary and appreciated by many species, such as *Pyrrhulina vittata.

Danio malabarcus **works well in the upper and middle parts of the larger aquarium. Photo by H.-J. Richter.**

happen in a normal community aquarium with not too many fishes, or with more fishes when we can supply them with darker and quieter spots. It is different with *Copella arnoldi*, which will spawn outside the water, mostly on the cover glass. The male should also have a quiet spot in the aquarium where he can build a preserve, just like *Pyrrhulina* species. Large or small, they prefer spawning on a large leaf. The smaller species spawn on a leaf approximately 6 centimeters long and from 3 to 4 centimeters wide, while the larger ones use, of course, larger leaves. The leaves should also be strong enough. In the first place, the *Anubias* species are relevant as are *Echinodorus*, like *horizontalis*, *cordifolius* and such. These plants also have to grow in the right spot, which are somewhat away from places that are too often frequented by other fishes when they are swimming. These spots are somewhat away from the large swimming area. They are bordered with other plants. A cover glass is especially necessary and appreciated by

many species, for instance, the small *Pyrrhulina* species. Are those plants missing those tetras, or are they just situated at the wrong spot? The fish will swim around them without utilizing them.

These fish can be perfectly placed together with *Gasteropelecus maculatus*, but also with *Rivulus* species. These fish will swim throughout the entire

aquarium, but will spawn preferably just below the surface and even on the floating plants, like *Riccia fluitans*. They also use the roots, especially from, *Ceratopteris* species or the *Myriophyllum* garlands that grow along the surface. In this way, the plants have two functions. They serve as a light dimmer and as a spawning place.

Rasbora heteromorpha **can be found in much clearer water, but they are much less colorful. Photo by M. P. & C. Piednoir.**

Acknowledgment

This volume in the *Basic Domestic Pet Library* series was researched in part at the Ontario Veterinary college at the University of Guelph in Guelph, Ontario, and was published under the auspice of Dr. Herbert R. Axelrod.

A world-renown scientist, explorer, author, university professor, lecturer, and publisher, Dr. Axelrod is the best-known tropical fish expert in the world and the founder and chairman of T.F.H. Publications, Inc., the largest and most respected publisher of pet literature in the world. He has written 16 definitive texts on Ichthyology (including the bestselling *Handbook of Tropical Aquarium Fishes*), published more than 30 books on individual species of fish for the hobbyist, written hundreds of articles, and discovered hundreds of previously unknown species, six of which have been named after him.

Dr. Axelrod holds a Ph.D and was awarded an Honorary Doctor of Science degree by the University of Guelph, where he is now an adjunct professor in the Department of Zoology. He has served on the American Pet Products Manufacturers Association Board of Governors and is a member of the American Society of Herpetologists and Ichthyologists, the Biometric Society, the New York Zoological Society, the New York Academy of Sciences, the American Fisheries Society, the National Research Council, the National Academy of Sciences, and numerous aquarium societies around the world.

In 1977, Dr. Axelrod was awarded the Smithson Silver Medal for his ichthyological and charitable endeavors by the Smithsonian Institution. A decade later, he was elected an endowment member of the American Museum of Natural History and was named a life member of the James Smithson Society by the Smithsonian Associates' national board. He has donated in excess of $50 million in recent years to the American Museum of National History, the University of Guelph, and other institutions.

INDEX